Kananaskis Country Colours

Kananaskis Country Colours

Alberta's Rockies Wilderness

Mike Potter

LUMINOUS
COMPOSITIONS

LUMINOUS
COMPOSITIONS

Published by
Luminous Compositions
2815 Lionel Crescent SW, Calgary, Alberta, Canada T3E 6B1

e-mail: luminouscompositions@shaw.ca
www. luminouscompositions.com

Library and Archives Canada Cataloguing in Publication Data

Potter, Mike, 1954-
    Kananaskis Country colours: Alberta's Rockies wilderness

Includes bibliographical references.
ISBN 0-9780170-0-5

    1. Kananaskis Country (Alta.)--Pictorial works. 2. Natural history--Alberta--Kananaskis Country--Pictorial works. 3. Rocky Mountains, Canadian (B.C. and Alta.)--Pictorial works. 4. Wilderness areas--Alberta--Pictorial works. I. Title.

FC3695.K36P68 2006   508.7123'32   C2006-900800-0

Printed on recycled paper (100 lb Sterling Gloss with 10% post-consumer material) and bound by Friesens, Altona, Manitoba, Canada R0G 0B0

Photographs:
(Page 2--opposite title page) A November sunrise glows above--and is reflected upon--the frozen surface of Moose Pond in the Sibbald Flat area of the northern region of Kananaskis Country.
(Contents page opposite) September colours tinge the subalpine larches and grasses at Maude Lake in Peter Lougheed Provincial Park, with Mt. Maude rising above North Kananaskis Pass at the far end of the lake.

I dedicate this book to my wife Jane, who gave excellent advice and suggestions, who is a superb proof-reader, and whose love and support enabled me to complete this project.

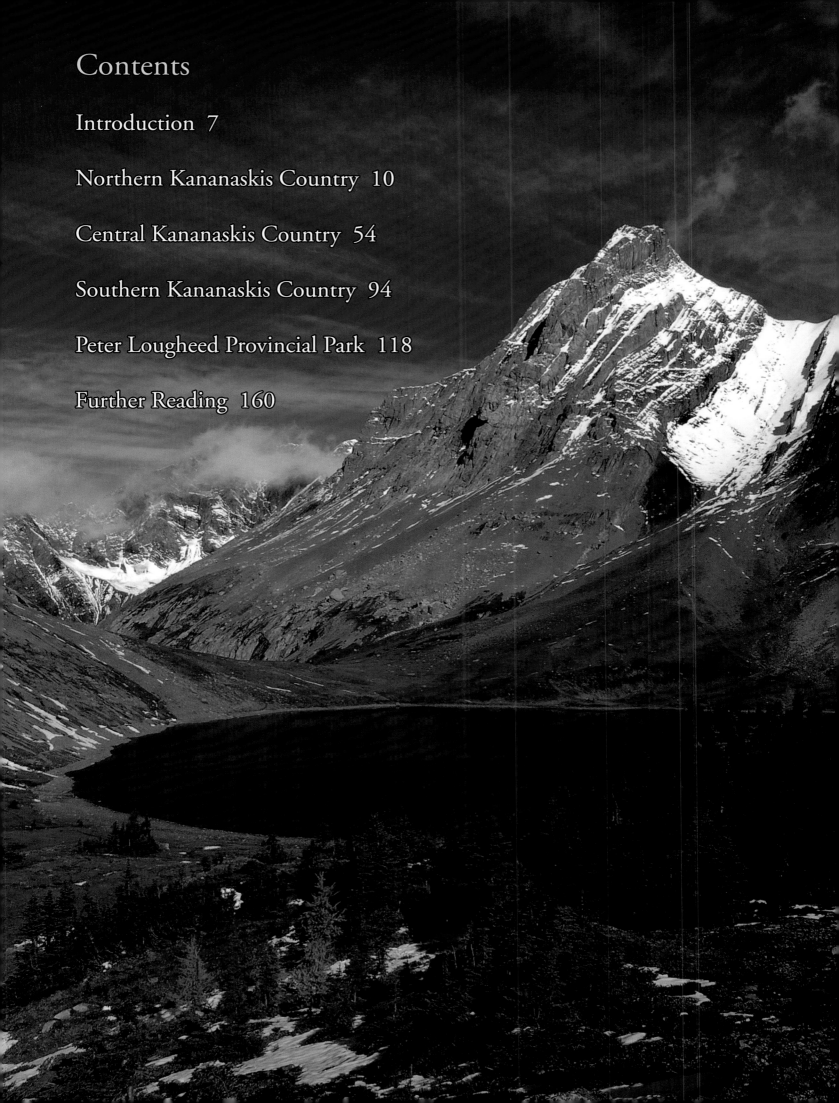

Contents

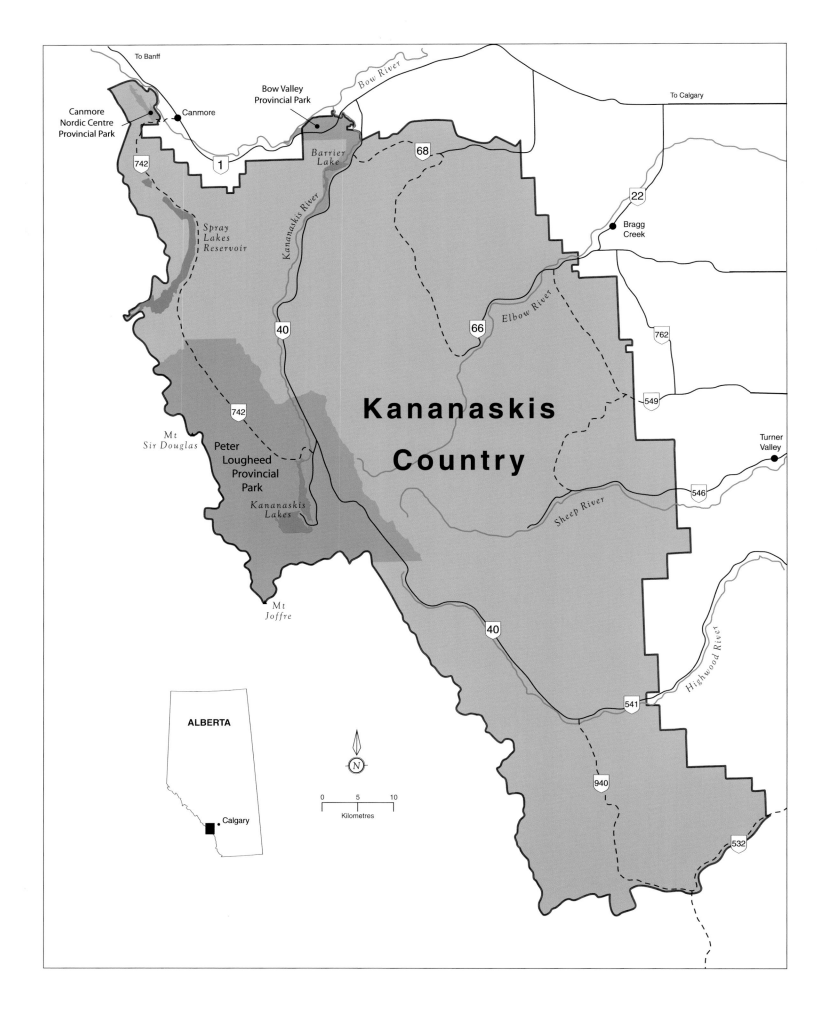

6 Kananaskis Country Colours

Introduction

Kananaskis Country, lying west and southwest of the city of Calgary, Alberta, is a vast multiple use area encompassing 4200 square kilometres (over 1600 square miles) of Canadian Rockies wilderness. Kananaskis Country holds within its boundaries a wide variety of habitats and a great diversity of wildlife. It also offers scope for a broad range of recreational activities, and acts as a refuge and place of solace for those seeking renewal in natural surroundings.

Kananaskis Country takes in portions of the foothills and the Front Ranges, east of the Main Ranges in the Canadian Rockies. Created and administered by the province of Alberta, Kananaskis Country protects a natural landscape that is much less well known than Banff National Park, which borders its northwestern edge.

Kananaskis Country presents a treasure trove of wilderness experiences. Many destinations in Kananaskis Country are easily accessible. For example, Elbow Falls cascade over a drop in the Elbow River less than 30 minutes drive from the urban concentration of Calgary.

Another illustration of the ease of approach to the delights of Kananaskis Country is the fact that Highway 40 (also known as Kananaskis Trail), which passes through its core, rates as the highest paved road in Canada. It travels over Highwood Pass, elevation 2206 metres (7236 ft), on the divide between the Highwood River and Kananaskis River watersheds.

The extensive network of roads in Kananaskis Country ranges from wide paved highways to narrow, winding gravel roads. These arteries allow for a quick approach to many places, yet there are still large areas of backcountry available to self-propelled adventurers. (Parts of most roads in Kananaskis Country are closed in winter to give wildlife such as elk and bighorn sheep breathing space on their cold season range.)

The name of Kananaskis Country looks like a tongue twister, but its pronunciation is easily mastered by breaking the word down phonetically: ka-na-nas-kis.

The name, originally bestowed on the Kananaskis River by John Palliser, leader of the 1857-1860 Palliser Expedition, honours a Native of the Cree people. He was a tough individual, for he is reported to have survived an axe blow to the head.

The name Kananaskis now also graces two passes at the headwaters of the river, two lakes (artificially enlarged) along its course, and a mountain range west of the river, as well as Kananaskis Country. (Kananaskis Country is often abbreviated as K Country.)

The establishment of Kananaskis Country took place in 1977, and it was officially dedicated on September 22, 1978. The development of facilities was thanks to revenues generated by oil and gas royalties in Alberta that had been put into the province's Heritage Fund. (Thus the extraction of those non-renewable resources contributed to the creation of this area where visitor's spirits can be renewed.)

Part of the motivation for protecting Kananaskis Country was to take some of the pressure off the national parks, especially Banff, by providing other recreational opportunities for Albertans and out-of-province visitors. A distinction is that to date there is no entry fee to Kananaskis Country, unlike national parks.

Although the level of infrastructure is less than in national parks, a lot of money [both public and private] has been invested in facilities. These include campgrounds (frontcountry and backcountry), trails, visitor centres, interpretive theatres, picnic areas, cross-country and downhill ski areas, and commercial accommodation.

The program of interpretive events is an integral part of Kananaskis Country, for it was felt that providing opportunities for people to learn about the environment would help them to value and appreciate the land and its living things. In particular, the evening programs given by Kananaskis Country staff are celebrated for their enthusiasm and creativity.

The large area of Kananaskis Country incorporates a number of provincial parks, of which the best known is Peter Lougheed Provincial Park (formerly Kananaskis Provincial Park) in its southwestern corner. Bow Valley Provincial Park and Canmore Nordic Centre Provincial Park lie in the northern part of Kananaskis Country, accessible via the Trans-Canada Highway. Other units of Kananaskis Country include Spray Valley Provincial Park, Sheep River Provincial Park, Bow Valley Wildland Provincial Park, Elbow-Sheep Wildland Provincial Park, and Bluerock Wildland Provincial Park.

The boundaries of this welter of parks are rather arbitrary, so this book will refer to all of them except Peter Lougheed Provincial Park as simply Kananaskis Country. I have instead divided it into three areas defined by natural features.

The northern region covers all the area north of the Elbow River in the east and north of Peter Lougheed Provincial Park in the west. Kananaskis Country's central region includes the Elbow River, takes in the Sheep River valley, and extends down to the Highwood River. The southern region encompasses the Highwood River and all the area south of it. As mentioned above, for presentation in this book, Peter Lougheed Provincial Park constitutes the fourth region of Kananaskis Country.

I have a connection with Kananaskis Country dating back some 20 years. In 1986, I began work as a park interpreter (naturalist) with Parks Canada in neighbouring Banff National Park. Although I initially stayed mostly within the Banff park boundaries as I explored the Rockies, I was already venturing into Kananaskis Country by that first winter. I signed up for a telemark skiing course with mountain guide Daniel Bonzi, based in Canmore, and part of the instruction took place in the renowned Burstall Pass area.

I have gained intimate knowledge of Kananaskis Country over the years, engaging in a gamut of outdoor pursuits such as hiking, backpacking, ridgewalking, off-trail scrambling, alpine climbing, rock climbing, cross-country skiing, ski mountaineering, birdwatching, and photography. Curiosity has led me to visit most major valleys in Kananaskis Country, and has also prompted me to reach the summits of over 100 named peaks to date in Kananaskis Country.

My knowledge of Kananaskis Country has been particularly enhanced in the course of researching and writing some of my previous Luminous Compositions books. The first of my books to deal directly with Kananaskis Country was *Central Rockies Wildflowers*, published in 1996 and reprinted in 2005. (Kananaskis Country is a major part of the Central Rockies Ecosystem, which also includes Banff, Kootenay, and Yoho national parks.) Many of the photographs in *Central Rockies Wildflowers* were taken in Kananaskis Country, particularly in Bow Valley Provincial Park.

My next book was *Central Rockies Placenames* (1997), which includes the fascinating story behind the names of the geographic features of Kananaskis Country. In 1997, I also edited and contributed to another title in the 'Pack-it' Pocket Guide series, *Central Rockies Mammals* by John Marriott (who had been a Parks Canada colleague).

The preparation of my next two books saw me in Kananaskis Country for lots of 'on the ground' research. Of the 82 outings described in *Fire Lookout Hikes in the Canadian Rockies* (1998), 10 are to fire lookouts in Kananaskis Country. What got me rolling on that project was going up to Barrier Lake Lookout in 1995 and meeting observer Chip McCullough, who opened my eyes to the intriguing stories connected with fire lookouts.

Ridgewalks in the Canadian Rockies (2001, revised 2003) entailed much off-trail exploration of Kananaskis Country as I scoped out its many alluring ridgewalks. Fully half of the over 140 routes in that book fall within Kananaskis Country, among them many of my favourites.

The most recent predecessor to this book is the photographic portfolio *White Wilderness: The Canadian Rockies in Winter* (2001). As can be imagined, it features images from Kananaskis Country, among them one from that first destination of mine, Burstall Pass.

I have also become familiar with areas of Kananaskis Country through GPS fieldwork and trail descriptions done for Gem Trek Publishing, particularly for their "Highwood & Cataract Creek, South Kananaskis Country" map first published in 2003.

Kananaskis Country is a multiple use area, which means that wildlife and habitat protection, and outdoor recreation, are not the only factors in its management. Other activities do take place in Kananaskis Country, subject to legislation. These include hunting, motorized use in designated zones, cattle grazing, logging, and oil and gas exploration and extraction.

These uses can affect wildlife and wilderness enthusiasts, so be prepared for less-than-pristine experiences in some areas. Clearly, parts of Kananaskis Country do not have the same level of ecological integrity as national parks; however, the drawbacks in this regard tend to be balanced by a generally lower degree of development and by lower levels of visitation. The Kananaskis Country Recreation Policy states that no further large-scale development proposals, such as golf courses, ski hills, and large accommodation centres, will be entertained. Any development must not cause serious or irreversible damage to the ecosystem.

A prime function of Kananaskis Country is to provide clean air and water. Clean air is essential in a time of global warming, and the extensive forests of Kananaskis Country contribute significantly to carbon reduction. Watershed protection benefits many downstream users, including residents of Calgary, and farmers and ranchers on lands to the east and south.

Those interested in becoming involved in efforts to maintain the calibre of the wilderness of Kananaskis Country can support organizations such as The Friends of Kananaskis Country (www. kananaskis.org), the Canadian Parks and Wilderness Society (www.cpaws.org), and the Yellowstone to Yukon Conservation Initiative (www.y2y.net).

Acknowledgements

I would like to thank Diana Cooper, Executive Director of The Friends of Kananaskis Country, for her encouragement. Kathy Wilcox of the Friends made a welcome suggestion.

Kananaskis Country staff provided lots of helpful information and assistance, especially Steve Donelon, Duane Fizor, Wayne Grams, and Carol Mehling.

Ben Gadd, who wrote the invaluable *Handbook of the Canadian Rockies*, answered a geology question. John Acorn ("The Nature Nut") helped with insect and spider identification. I salute the work of Ben, John, and the other authors listed in Further Reading on p. 160.

Scott Jevons of Geoworks, Canmore, produced the map on p. 6.

Jim Beckel and Brad Schmidt of Friesens again helped me with many printing questions.

John Blum and Isabelle Lemelin of Alpine Book Peddlers, Canmore, gave valued feedback on book design.

My wife Jane contributed to all aspects of this book (see the dedication on p. 4).

Green rolling ridges of the Mackay Hills lie in the foreground of this view southeast from the upper slopes of the peak known as The Wedge. Beyond rise grey limestone ridges of Fisher Peak, still snow-flecked in early July.

The northern region of Kananaskis Country covers all the land north of the Highway 66 corridor in the east and north of Peter Lougheed Provincial Park in the west. This region takes in a variety of landforms, including the low elevation montane zone, forested foothills, and craggy mountaintops. It supports a range of life from chipmunks to grizzly bears, from red-winged blackbirds to golden eagles, from yellow lady's slippers to kittentails.

The order of presentation is first the northern district as travelling west along the Trans-Canada Highway. This includes Bow Valley Provincial Park with its many wildflowers, boisterous Heart Creek, and intriguing Grassi Lakes in Canmore Nordic Centre Provincial Park below the ramparts of Mt. Rundle.

Next comes the often-overlooked Jumping-pound/Sibbald area of the foothills, accessible via Highway 68. Here you will experience inviting aspen stands, especially attractive in fall, and you may observe some surprising bird species.

Then we go south along Highway 40 in the Kananaskis Valley, with such landmarks as Mt. Lorette, Mt. Allan, Ribbon Creek, and Mt. Kidd. Farther south in this district lie features such as the peak called The Wedge, Fortress Ridge, and Galatea Creek with three turquoise lakes at the head of its northwest branch. Watch (or join!) whitewater enthusiasts in action on the Kananaskis River, or make a winter visit to frozen Troll Falls.

Finally come the more remote haunts along the gravel Smith-Dorrien/Spray Trail (Highway 742) south of Canmore, which grants access to outings such as The Big Sister, Old Goat Glacier, Mt. Sparrowhawk, and Tent Ridge. Other possibilities include the hike to enticingly named West Wind Pass or a workout on the cross-country ski trails near Mt. Shark.

This northern region of Kananaskis Country exhibits much diversity and provides extensive scope for exploration.

(Above) Tall spires of elephanthead reveal the derivation of its name from a fancied resemblance to a pachyderm with big ears and curved trunk. This species is found in marshy situations.

(Right) Blooming in early summer, the vibrant colours of calypso orchids are particularly welcome after the monochromatic hues of winter. These tropical-looking wildflowers grow in shady forest. Their exotic appearance combines with a fragrant aroma, which each year attract inexperienced bumblebees that do not at first realize there is no nectar to reward their pollination services. They 'move on' but the job gets done for the orchids.

(Above) Large and colourful, the western wood lily grows throughout the foothills. It has recovered from heavy picking in earlier times.

(Right) A male pine grosbeak feeds on seeds of tall larkspur in the fall. This bird got access to this food item by landing near the top of the stem to bend it over, then sidling along it to reach the reward. With their short, stout bills, grosbeaks fill the niche of parrots in Canada.

(Above) Yellow lady's slipper stands out even among its showy relatives in the orchid family. Its brilliant pouch and enticing fragrance act as beacons to pollinating bees. This species can be located in damp low elevation habitats such as in Bow Valley Provincial Park.

(Left top) Two damselflies in the process of mating alight on a wildflower near Middle Lake in Bow Valley Provincial Park. Damselflies are smaller relatives of dragonflies.

(Left bottom) The purple streaking on the lower three petals of Western Canada violet serves to guide pollinators to nectar.

(Above) The long buttressed ridge of Mt. Rundle towers above Canmore Nordic Centre Provincial Park. The superb facilities of the park have seen action as the venue for Olympic and World Cup cross-country ski events.

(Left top) This spring provides much of the flow in Heart Creek. It is located beyond the end of the maintained trail.

(Left bottom) River beauty, a smaller relative of fireweed, often grows along the banks of watercourses in Kananaskis Country.

(Top) A Native pictograph on a large boulder in the canyon above Grassi Lakes. Orange lichens add their own pattern to the rock.

(Bottom) Leaves of Labrador tea {which turn colour as they fade} photographed on the Grassi Lakes trail. Pioneers made a hot beverage with this plant.

(Right) A small shrub in fall raiment, complemented by the clear green waters of the lower Grassi Lake.

Grassi Lakes

The hike on the interpretive trail to the colourful Grassi Lakes near Canmore is a short one and deservedly popular. The trail starts above the Nordic Centre and takes a mostly gradual line, passing through forest whose understory includes Labrador tea and shrubby cinquefoil. There are views of the impressive waterfall issuing from the lakes.

The two Grassi Lakes are small and shallow but very colourful, their clear waters exhibiting shades of green and blue. There is a plaque on a rock at the lower lake for Lawrence Grassi, after whom the lakes are named. Grassi, an Italian-born Canmore coal miner, was also a mountaineer, guide, and trailbuilder among whose projects was the original trail to these lakes (his work has since been flooded). Out of sight above the lakes and beyond Ha Ling Peak and Miners Peak is the long massif of Mt. Lawrence Grassi, also named in honour of this renowned pioneer.

Taking a steep, loose trail above the upper lake leads into a rocky canyon where a large boulder features several historic Native rock paintings (pictographs). Created in red ochre, they are located quite high up below an overhang.

The canyon holds other unexpected delights, including strawberry blite, a rare wildflower that originated in Eurasia which has arrowhead-shaped leaves and bright red fruit. You might also sight a pika {see photograph and sidebar p. 125}.

(Above) Osprey are fairly common in Kananaskis Country, but it was a surprise to come across this one perched above Sibbald Creek across from Highway 68. It didn't seem a likely place to catch the fish that are an osprey's main prey, but then anglers usually have secret spots. {And, come to think of it, Sibbald Meadows Pond was nearby.}

(Right) A boreal owl found in the Sibbald Flat area stares wide-eyed at me as I take its photograph. This species, though not often seen at its daytime roosts, does allow close approach once located. As was the case here, this species is most often sighted in spring, when it nests. The three to six eggs are laid in a tree cavity, often one excavated by woodpeckers but no longer in use by those birds. This image is at life size.

(Above) Anthocyanins produced from residual sugars in fall tint the leaves of fireweed flame red, although other foliage remains green.

(Right) A northern flicker perches at the entrance to its nest cavity. This bird has the red nape and black malar (moustache) stripe of a male of the yellow-shafted subspecies. The red-shafted subspecies also occurs in Kananaskis Country, as well as hybrids of the two.

(Above and right) Whitewater canoeists and kayakers practise their skills on the Kananaskis River below Barrier Dam. The volume at sites such as Widow Maker and Santa Claus fluctuates under human management. The flows allow paddlers, including rafters, to enjoy the rush of wild water in this section of Bow Valley Provincial Park.

(Above) A snow flurry creates a timeless tableau of a group of bighorn sheep ewes and lambs. Although inclement conditions present challenges for photography, they can yield evocative results.

(Right top) Winter transforms the waters of Kananaskis Country, in this instance freezing Troll Falls near Ribbon Creek into turquoise ice. Adjacent seepages also form pillars in the cold.

(Right bottom) A filigree of rime crystals makes an abstract sculpture of a cow parsnip stalk.

(Above) Rock pillars tower above a hiker on the Centennial Ridge trail, the highest maintained trail in Kananaskis Country. The summit of Mt. Allan rises on the right, while peaks of Mt. Lougheed rise higher still to the left.

(Right top) Alpine spring beauty is a rare denizen of the high country, related to the more common western spring beauty of lower elevations.

(Right bottom) This view from Mt. Collembola leads over the north ridge of Mt. Allan to {left to right} a peak of Mt. Lougheed, The Three Sisters, and Mt. Rundle in the distance.

(Following pages left) A September snowfall embroiders tall conifers on the Barrier Bluffs, above Barrier Lake on its east side.

(Following pages right) The branches of a trembling aspen turned golden in autumn frame a view of Mt. Lorette in the Kananaskis Valley. The famed golden eagle migration recognized by Peter Sherrington and Des Allen in 1992 passes above this landmark.

31 Kananaskis Country Colours

(Above) Dramatic folds in the rock of Mt. Kidd {on the right} and especially its south peak testify to the powerful forces of mountain building that created the Rockies.

(Left) Wedge Pond is a photographer's paradise, especially in autumn when the deciduous trees that ring it metamorphose into golden shades. Looking west from the pond, the skyline peaks are The Fortress, with its craggy profile, and Gusty Peak, with Fortress Ridge below.

(Top) This rare perspective from the slopes of Bogart Tower shows Third Memorial Lake, with its unusual peninsula. In the upper left is the cairn honouring those lost in a series of plane crashes: tragic events that gave rise to the names of the three lakes at the head of North Ribbon Creek.

(Bottom) Alpine hawksbeard has a long taproot to anchor it among rocks.

(Right) This vantage from near North Buller Pass shows Ribbon Lake and the south peak of Mt. Kidd. Guinns Pass lies just out of sight in the upper right.

Ribbon Creek

The trail up Ribbon Creek, lying deep between limestone ramparts, provides for a variety of options, from a short stroll up the valley to a backpacking trip to Ribbon Lake and beyond.

Tall Ribbon Falls are a spectacular highlight, with a backcountry campground at their base. To continue farther, it's necessary to negotiate a cliffband (chains provided). From the upper backcountry campground at colourful Ribbon Lake, more choices present themselves in the shape of a trip over Guinns Pass into Galatea Creek or over one of two passes into Buller Creek.

Of course, there are still other possibilities, such as the rough trail up to Memorial Lakes or the daunting off-trail scramble of Mt. Bogart (named not for an actor, but for geologist D. Bogart Dowling).

(Above) Upper Galatea Lake shimmers in the sun at the headwaters of Galatea Creek. These alpine surroundings can be readily visited from a base at the Lillian Lake back-country campground.

(Right top) An island of purple saxifrage has become established in a rocky crevice. This wildflower belongs to the genus *Saxifraga*, whose name means "rock-breaker," for its members secrete minute amounts of acid that help to break down rock into soil. Thus purple saxifrage can be said to enhance its habitat, which helps it survive in the high cold places where it lives. The orange growth on the rock is an *Xanthoria* lichen. Lichens are symbiotic (mutually beneficial) associations of a fungus and an algae. I'll always remember one of my first days as a park interpreter, when I realized the creativity of the job extended to groaner puns after a colleague returning for his third summer introduced himself as having taken a 'lichen' to the park while plunking down a rock encrusted with these organisms of ancient lineage.

(Right bottom) Be alert to the presence of northern sweetvetch (also called purple hedysarum), whose roots are an important part of the diet of grizzly bears.

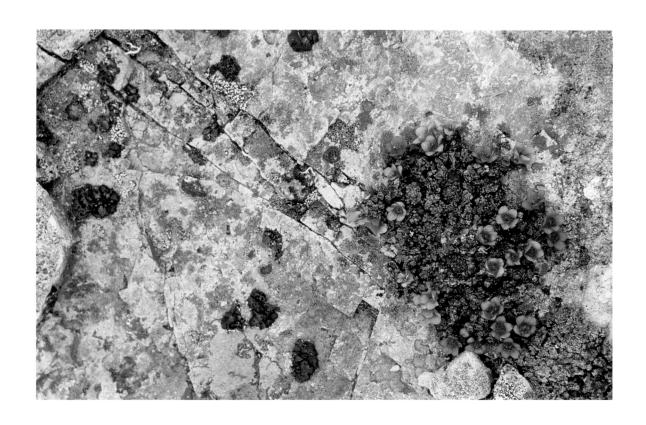

39 Kananaskis Country Colours

(Above) Clouds wreath the Opal Range as a storm clears. I witnessed this stirring scene in evening light from the Peninsula day use area at the north end of Lower Kananaskis Lake.

(Right) A photographic bouquet of wildflowers {clockwise from upper left}: kittentails, an unusual species mostly found at higher elevations; shooting star, a widespread member of the primrose family; alpine forget-me-not with its sky-blue blossoms; and common harebell, which despite its fragile appearance and thin stem is tenacious, often found in bloom well into September.

(Above) A porcupine portrait shows the long curved claws these mammals use for getting up trees, and the long yellow guard hairs. Porcupines are often unfairly maligned. Although they will gnaw on objects such as leather boots and wooden paddles for salt, it is an easy matter to store such gear properly. And porcupines don't throw their quills like miniature javelins, contrary to some notions. They must make contact with their barbed armour for it to lodge, a feat they can accomplish by lashing about with the tail.

(Left top) A clouded sulphur butterfly, with delicate pink and green colouring, rests on a fading common harebell.

(Left bottom) A mourning cloak butterfly feeds on willow catkins in spring. Surprisingly, adults of this species can be found any day of the year, weather permitting. They overwinter as adults, hibernating in hollow trees.

(Above) Clouds drift over the summits of Windtower (foreground) and a peak of Mt. Lougheed, as seen from the slopes of the mountain known as Rimwall. Mt. Lougheed was originally named by Eugene Bourgeau of the 1857-1860 Palliser Expedition, who called it Windy Mountain, and was referred to as Wind Mountain by George Dawson of the Geological Survey of Canada in 1886. The present name was bestowed in 1928 after James A. Lougheed, a prominent Alberta lawyer and politician, and a grandfather of Peter Lougheed—who as Premier of Alberta oversaw the creation of Kananaskis Country.

(Left top) Alberta is "Wild Rose Country" and Kananaskis Country harbours many of these wild-flowers, renowned for their large, colourful blooms and strong fragrance. See p. 66 for a photograph of the fruit of this species, known as rosehips.

(Left bottom) A small island of moss campion persists on bare rock on the upper slopes of The Big Sister. This favourite among wildflower enthusiasts grows only in the alpine zone, where it can take ten or more years to first flower. Its island-like growth form protects it from desiccating wind, and collects wind-blown particles of earth to slowly build up soil. A deep taproot anchors the plant and allows it to obtain water in what are usually quick-draining locations. Despite these adaptations, moss campion leads a tenuous existence, making its fragile beauty all the more reward when you venture into its habitat.

(Above) An early morning hike to Old Goat Glacier near the north end of Spray Lakes Reservoir yielded this alpine scene. The sun is still low enough that it casts into silhouette the slopes of the ridge nestling the glacier on the east.

(Left top) Sawwort is a pioneering species on stony ground.

(Left bottom) Bladder campion (*Silene uralensis*) is able to thrive on the dry, rocky moraines of the Old Goat Glacier. This wildflower is also known as Chinese lantern due to its distinctive shape; the purple petals grow at the mouth of the ridged calyx. (This is a native species, unlike related *S. cucubalus*, also named bladder campion.)

48 Kananaskis Country Colours

(Above) An incongruous sight: bright green moss thrives amid extensive alpine boulderfields below the summit of Mt. Sparrowhawk.

(Left top) The prow of Reads Tower rears high, as seen on the off-trail scrambling route up Mt. Sparrowhawk. Such landforms illustrate differential erosion, in which softer rock disappears while layers more resistant to forces such as wind, rain, and frost persist.

(Left bottom) Spotted saxifrage, which indeed sports spotted petals, is a high country delight.

Mt. Sparrowhawk

The off-trail scramble to the summit of Mt. Sparrowhawk (3121 m/10,240 ft) involves an elevation gain of some 1350 m (4430 ft), but apart from this significant climb the outing does not present any great difficulty provided the route is snow-free.

Head up from the Sparrowhawk day use area on the Smith-Dorrien/Spray Trail (Highway 742), veering left from the trail up Sparrowhawk Creek to gain Reads Ridge. You lose some hard-earned height to pass below Reads Tower to its north, then scramble up onto the broad west slopes of the mountain.

It's a long haul up to a saddle south of the summit block, enlivened by occasional islands of emerald green moss supported by snowmelt amid vast expanses of shattered grey rocks. The grade on the final section to the summit steepens; this part should be dry. The vistas from the top are superlative, highlights being the four peaks of Mt. Lougheed, and, far down to the southeast, two of the three Memorial Lakes nestled below the steep eastern cliffs of Mt. Bogart.

(Above) The wind catches the 'horns' (feather tufts) of a great horned owl nesting in a trembling aspen. This species, which is a year-round resident, is the provincial bird of Alberta.

(Left) A northern goshawk perches on a trembling aspen in the foot-hills zone. This raptor (hunting species) is the largest of the *Accipiter* genus, whose members have short wings and long tails for maneuvering at speed through trees as they pursue prey—usually smaller birds. The white stripe above the adult's red eye is diagnostic (a distinctive identifying feature).

(Above) Tent Ridge makes for an excellent ridgewalk, as amply evident in this vista looking south along the west arm over the linking ridge and the east arm of the horseshoe. The cluster of serrated summits on the skyline includes Mt. Birdwood on the far right.

(Left top) The author rambling on the west arm of Tent Ridge, with views north over Spray Lakes Reservoir to the mountains beyond. The two snowy peaks on the right are Old Goat Mountain {in bright sunshine} and Mt. Nestor, both situated on the boundary between Banff National Park and Kananaskis Country.

(Left bottom) Dwarf larkspur ekes out a niche on rocky ground.

Rock outcrops dot aptly named High Rock Ridge near Sullivan Pass in the seldom-travelled eastern part of the central region of Kananaskis Country. The long southeast ridge of Junction Mountain rises above grassy slopes green at the height of summer.

Kananaskis Country's central region encompasses the Elbow River, takes in the Sheep River Valley, and extends down to the Highwood River. It has many clear-running creeks and rivers, several pristine lakes, and vast tracts of wild country with abundant wildlife.

The valley of the Elbow River is easily reached from Calgary via Highway 66, with Elbow Falls a perennially popular destination all year long. Moose Mountain and Prairie Mountain represent fine hiking choices, while one option for mountain bikers is the old fire road that leads all the way up to the headwaters at Elbow Lake. Backpackers can head up the valley of the Little Elbow River and beyond.

Perhaps because no road leads all the way up it, the valley of the Sheep River is less well known than its neighbour to the north. However, this drainage is a gem of Kananaskis Country. Reached via Highway 546 west of the town of Turner Valley, it holds extensive aspen parklands in the east and seldom-travelled terrain leading to its headwaters. And yes, you are quite likely to see wild sheep here, especially from the Bighorn viewpoint.

The part of this region south of the Sheep River takes in a large expanse of land on its eastern side that is hard to get into, including the watershed of Flat Creek with historical connotations. On the other hand, this region includes eyecatching places north of the Highwood River, such as the Bull Creek Hills and Mist Ridge, that are easy to visit thanks to Highways 541 and 40 west of Longview. Worth visiting even if you're not into angling are the Picklejar Lakes (the story goes that fish were so plentiful they could be caught with, you guessed it, picklejars)—these four small lakes are set in a rugged basin that makes for a good day hike.

This central region of Kananaskis Country features readily accessible highlights, while embracing a few secrets that require more effort to see.

(Above) The jade water of the Elbow River pulses over rocks just upstream of Elbow Falls. The name of the river derives from a pronounced bend in the river {now inundated by Calgary's Glenmore Reservoir}. Serendipitously, the Elbow is a tributary of the Bow River.

(Left top) Elbow Falls roar over the drop at the height of their summer volume in late June. The full flow of the Elbow River, the Little Elbow, and many tributaries races down, reflecting the extent of snowmelt and recent rains. Note that the rock at the lip of the falls is covered, whereas it is exposed in the two winter images on the next pages.

(Left bottom) These intriguing rock formations occur beside the Elbow River not far downstream of Elbow Falls.

Elbow River

The valley of the Elbow River tempts as the most easily reached part of Kananaskis Country from Calgary. A few minutes beyond the hamlet of Bragg Creek, Highway 66 gives access to a multitude of recreational opportunities.

Hikes such as Ranger Ridge, Moose Mountain with an active fire lookout, Prairie Mountain, and Powderface Ridge all beckon from along the road up the valley. Mountain biking, horseback riding, water sports, and fishing are possible, as well as quieter pursuits such as birdwatching and nature photography. Several frontcountry campgrounds and numerous picnic areas make for restful bases, whether for a week or for an hour.

From the confluence of the Little Elbow River with the Elbow, you can venture up either valley, for example hiking onto Nihahi Ridge and perhaps continuing along it on an off-trail scramble. Another option is to backpack to the Mount Romulus backcountry campground. This can serve as the base for an attempt to scramble up the peak of that name (requires a river crossing), or as a waypoint on a multi-day trip over Tombstone Pass. From there a circuit can be made down the Elbow River back to the start, or you can continue to the headwaters at Elbow Lake and exit via Elbow Pass to Highway 40.

The narrow, twisting, gravel Powderface Trail runs north from the end of Highway 66 through to Highway 68 and the Sibbald area. Along the way are trailheads for popular outings on Jumpingpound Mountain and Cox Hill.

Whatever your choices, the Elbow Valley will reward with enjoyable experiences.

(Above) A recent snowfall mantles the surroundings of Elbow Falls in winter.

(Left) A time exposure on a night with full moon illumination paints a winter scene at Elbow Falls. With the shutter open for more than a minute, the movement of the stars is recorded as bright tracks.

(Above) A beaver gnaws on a small branch, feeding on the cambium layer. Beavers use the larger branches of trees that they have felled with their sharp teeth to build their dams and lodges. Rocks and mud are also incorporated as building materials into their structures, which have earned beavers the nickname 'engineers of the wild.' Beavers do not hibernate. They are active through winter, feeding under the ice on food supplies that they set aside in the fall.

(Left top) An adult Canada goose and goslings parade by at Beaver Ponds. The young are precocial: ready to leave the nest within a day or so of birth. They are able to swim almost immediately, and master flight at the age of about 60 days.

(Left bottom) A red squirrel pauses with a cone in its mouth. Note the long toes, an adaptation for climbing the trees that are its primary refuge. Squirrels do spend a fair amount of time down on the ground, and even underground in burrows in and beneath their middens {refuse heaps of discarded scales}. They nest in their burrows and shelter there during very cold weather. Squirrels are dextrous in handling cones, rotating them like corn-on-the-cob and dropping the scales as they procure the tiny seeds at their bases. These small mammals are vocal and ubiquitous year round in Kananaskis Country.

(Above) The author's wife strides along the northwest arm of Prairie Mountain. The hike to the summit is a popular early season warm-up, beginning at the Elbow Falls trailhead. To the north across the valley of Canyon Creek lie the high ridges of Moose Mountain, on whose top sits a fire lookout. As the name suggests, the flatlands to the east are visible from Prairie Mountain.

(Right top) A sweeping vista unveils from the upper slopes of Mt. Romulus, including this portion of the Opal Range. Mt. Blane stands as the prominent peak; the abrupt feature to its left is known as The Blade.

(Right bottom) The remnants of an August snowfall linger on the summit block of sheer-sided Mt. Romulus. Neighbouring Mt. Remus rises to the east, its name also originating somewhat obscurely in the classical story of twin brothers who founded the city of Rome.

63 Kananaskis Country Colours

(Above) False Solomon's seal, a member of the lily family, sports zigzag stems. At the end of summer, the small fragrant white flowers transform into a cluster of reddish berries, sometimes speckled with purple.

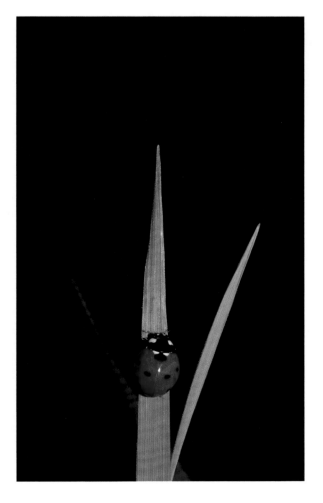

(Left) A ladybeetle {also called ladybugs} climbs a blade of grass. These insects mostly eat aphids.

(Far left) Star-flowered Solomon's seal exhibits elegant symmetry in its leaves. This member of the lily family is widespread at lower elevations.

(Above) The bright red fruit and bur-gundy leaves of this bunchberry show that it is fall. Also known as dwarf dog-wood, this species thrives on the floor of shady coniferous forests.

(Right) The colour of the berries of baneberry in autumn can be red or white. As the name suggests, all parts of this plant are poisonous. This spe-cies belongs to the buttercup family.

(Left) Bright red rosehips form in fall on wild rose, the provincial flower of Alberta (as commemorated on license plates). The large pink blossoms ex-ude a heady perfume in the summer, so be sure to take time to "stop and smell the roses."

(Above) Although the warm winds known as chinooks blow through frequently, there are spells of good cross-country skiing in the Sheep River Valley. It is the generally mild temperatures and usual lack of snow, though, that make this area such good winter range for wildlife.

(Left top) A group of bighorn rams rests in a meadow in the aptly-named Sheep River Valley. Visitors to Kananaskis Country often overlook this valley west of the small town of Turner Valley (partly because the road into it dead-ends) but it is well worth visiting, not least for wildlife. Beside bighorn sheep, the larger mammals that are often seen include white-tailed deer, mule deer, elk, and coyote. Other possibilities include cougar, grizzly bear, black bear, red fox, moose, and striped skunk.

(Left bottom) The remains of a bighorn sheep give mute testimony to the natural drama of predation and survival. A cougar made this winter kill, while a suite of creatures including coyotes, ravens, and magpies have benefited as well.

(Above) Thunderclouds build up over the Sheep River Valley. Summer afternoons regularly provide the chance to observe this impressive natural phenomenon, and later there is likely to be refreshing rain.

(Right top) Low hills near the Sandy McNabb campground in the Sheep River Valley allow for enjoyable rambling throughout the year.

(Right bottom) A field of flowers on the South Gorge Creek hiking trail includes low larkspur and three-flowered avens ('prairie smoke').

(Above) A male blue grouse displays. Purplish skin is briefly re-vealed as feathers puff out when the courting bird makes soft hoots by inflating and deflating two pouches on either side of the neck. As this photograph documents, the colour of the patches of skin on the head, called eye combs, can alternate between red and yellow (this image illustrates the transition). Blue grouse are the largest of the three species of grouse in the Canadian Rockies. {See photograph of ruffed grouse to the right, and one of spruce grouse on p. 103.}

(Right top) A male ruffed grouse raises the collar-like 'ruff' after which the species is named (note the iridescence in the feath-ers of the ruff). The drumming of breeding male ruffed grouse fills the air in spring and early summer: the sound is due to rap-id movement of the wings.

(Right bottom) A male American kestrel perches on a road sign in the Sheep River Valley. This diminutive member of the falcon family used to be referred to as "sparrowhawk," but it mostly feeds on insects such as grasshoppers. Kestrels often hover be-fore dropping onto prey.

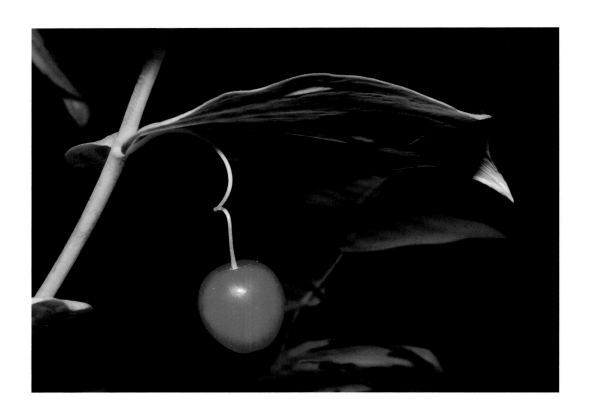

74 Kananaskis Country Colours

(Above) Red paintbrush and sticky purple geranium sometimes grow in close proximity. Both these species have relatives of different colours.

(Left top) The derivation of the name of twisted stalk is illustrated in this image of one of the berries that forms from small yellow-green flowers with curved petals. This member of the lily family occurs in dense montane and subalpine woodlands.

(Left bottom) This is the reverse side of the usual view of brown-eyed Susan (wild gaillardia), as seen on pages 84--85. This photograph is from the Bluerock interpretive trail at the end of Highway 549.

(Above) The golden colour of trembling aspens signals the fall season. Aspens often grow in groves of genetically identical trees that form by propagation along the roots. The leaves on their thin, flat stalks do indeed vibrate in even the lightest wind.

(Left top) Fireweed grows among trembling aspens in the Sheep River Valley. This tall wildflower establishes itself soon after fires, thus the common name. It also thrives in other disturbed areas, such as avalanche paths and roadsides. Fireweed, the floral emblem of the Yukon Territory, is widespread throughout the region of the Yellowstone to Yukon Conservation Initiative. Kananaskis Country is a vital part of this visionary endeavour.

(Left bottom) Wild bergamot, also known as horsemint, features large pink blossoms. This species has the square stem, opposite leaves, and notable fragrance that are typical of members of the mint family.

(Top) At times of high volume, the Sheep River presents challenging whitewater runs for experienced kayakers. Vertically tilted strata stand out in the canyon below Tiger Jaw Falls.

(Bottom) Sheep River Falls have allure even at low water, such as in this October image.

(Right) Although getting there entails a ford of the Sheep River and involves a mundane hike along Junction Creek, these graceful cascades certainly make the outing worthwhile.

(Above) Icicles festoon a cave on the summit ridge of Bluerock Mountain. This photograph was taken in mid-July, showing how variable the weather can be even during summer in the Rockies.

(Right) The view east down the Sheep River Valley from the Rickerts Pass junction includes the less frequently seen west and north aspects of the cliff known as Gibraltar. {This is the eastern outlier of Gibraltar Mountain.} The low black pile in the left foreground harkens back to the coal mines that once operated in the vicinity.

The Headwaters of the Sheep River

I lived in the small town of Turner Valley for over four years, and frequently enjoyed wandering in the Sheep River Valley to the west. But it wasn't until I moved away from Turner Valley that I finally made a pilgrimage to the headwaters of the Sheep on a backpacking trip.

An old road leads west from the end of Highway 546 near the Bluerock campgrounds, so it is easy travel. I pass by the cliff known as Gibraltar, whose sheer east face is a local landmark, and make a quick dash to revisit Rickerts Pass at the north end of Mist Ridge.

Continuing upvalley, I have a look at historic Dennings Cabin, then set up camp near Burns Creek. Next morning, I head up to Burns Lake, passing an impressive waterfall en route. Pushing onward from the lake, I forge cross-country up onto the open Rae Creek Hills, which give an excellent overview of the surroundings—including the headwaters of the Sheep.

Later that day I venture in that direction, meeting a park ranger on patrol and passing the camp of an equestrian party. I set up a camp near the Sheep Lakes that feed the river, and stay there two nights while I check out the surrounding area. A highlight is the visit the next day to small but scenic Lake Rae, situated below the steep cliffs of an outlier of Mt. Rae and located in the zone of subalpine larch (my favourite tree species in the Rockies).

My exit is via Elbow Pass to Highway 40, taking me beside the headwaters of the Elbow River at Elbow Lake with its popular backcountry campground.

(Above) Early morning light shines on the south peak of Tombstone Mountain, seen from near the Sheep Lakes.

(Left) Rock jasmine is a fragrant member of the primrose family, often found at great heights.

(Right) Tiny Lake Rae nestles beneath high cliffs of the northern outlier of Mt. Rae. Snow released by an avalanche still rests by the lakeshore in late June. The subalpine larch trees surrounding the lake indicate its high elevation setting, for this species grows only in the transition to the alpine zone.

(Following pages) Wildflowers dance in the wind in a meadow above Flat Creek. The most abundant species is brown-eyed Susan (wild gaillardia).

83 Kananaskis Country Colours

(Above) The famous Boundary Pine still stands near Grass Pass in the Bull Creek Hills. This limber pine with its windswept silhouette owes its name to author R.M. Patterson, who once had a ranch in the area and who wrote *The Buffalo Head*. That classic book first published in 1961 gives superb insights into the history, natural and human, of the Highwood River watershed. Limber pines can be identified by their clusters of needles growing in bunches of five, and by their large cones.

(Top) A weathered snag in the Bull Creek Hills acts as a nurse tree, sheltering new growth.

(Bottom) The small, serene cascades of photogenic Cat Creek Falls feed a clear green pool at the end of a short interpretive trail.

(Following pages) Even though they are close to Highway 40 (visible in this image), these tall pinnacles rising above the Highwood River Valley near Lineham Creek are not readily identifiable from below. Peaks on the continental divide, including Mt. Muir on the right and Mt. Armstrong to the right of the highest pinnacle, march off in the distance to the south.

89 Kananaskis Country Colours

(Above) Sweeping folds above Lineham Creek exhibit both anticline (arch-like) and syncline (concave upward) formations.

(Below) The delicate flowers of common bearberry later form red berries that are eaten by bears and many other creatures. Native people, who know this plant as kinnikinnik, also use the berries to make pemmican, a staple food.

(Right top) A September scene on Lineham Ridge: the vegetation has turned brown due to frosts at night, yet the sun beams down warmly during the day. Serried buttresses of the Highwood Range march above Lineham Creek. Mt. Head is the high peak right of centre; in the distance on the right are Mt. Burke and level Plateau Mountain.

(Right bottom) Elk often graze in the meadows above the Highwood River.

91 Kananaskis Country Colours

92 Kananaskis Country Colours

(Above) An elk antler cast off high on the crest of the southeastern out-lier of Mist Mountain. Mist Ridge lies in the mid-distance. The presence of this antler confirms the importance of the Highwood River Valley as win-ter range for elk, since antlers are dropped in February or March. Discarded antlers serve as sources of minerals for small rodents and snowshoe hares, which eventually gnaw away the bony 'hood ornaments' of the members of the deer family. (Antlers in the males of species such as elk, moose, and deer function primarily as indicators of evolutionary fitness for breeding.)

(Left top) The off-trail scramble of Mist Mountain via its northwest ridge re-veals this rugged terrain. The route does not traverse these pinnacles, rather heading to the top in the opposite direction.

(Left bottom) The view north along the northwest ridge of Mist Mountain takes in the other peaks of the Misty Range culminating in Mt. Rae. Appar-ent here is the abrupt transition from steep, craggy heights to gentler, grassy slopes that is so frequently found in Kananaskis Country.

Southern Kananaskis Country

A stand of trembling aspens reflects in a small beaver-created pond just off Highway 40 near the Highwood River. The reddish shrub in the foreground of this autumn scene is dwarf birch, less than one metre high but with the toothed leaves typical of the family.

The Highwood River and all the area south of it define the southern region of Kananaskis Country. Rolling forested slopes with increasingly deeper valleys culminate to the west in jagged limestone peaks arrayed along the continental divide. Here are high numbers of deer, elk, and bears (both black and grizzly) in a mostly untamed setting.

The northeastern part of this region is characterized by creeks including Cataract and Zephyr, graced with cascading waterfalls and Native pictographs. South of these are peaks such as Mt. Burke with its weathered and now empty fire lookout, and Plateau Mountain whose high level expanses escaped glaciation and so serve as habitat for rare plants.

Twisting, steep, and gravel, Highway 532 (known as Johnson Creek Trail) gives access from the east off Highway 22 to the southeastern corner of Kananaskis Country. Hiking highlights here are Hailstone Butte with an active fire lookout and Sentinel Peak overlooking Pekisko Creek.

West of Highway 940, the gravel Forestry Trunk Road that runs south from Highwood Junction, you find hiking destinations such as Raspberry Ridge, with another fire lookout, and Fording River Pass on the divide, gained via a long jaunt up Baril Creek.

Farther north, and reached off Highway 40, are such enticing spots as the Strawberry Hills, Hill of the Flowers, and Running Rain Lake. More rugged options include Carnarvon Lake (attaining it involves negotiating the cliffband below, on which a chain is affixed), Bishop Ridge, and the three tops of Odlum Ridge.

This south region is the most remote and (despite more evidence of such activities as grazing, logging, and oil and gas extraction) can claim the most off-the-beaten-track feel of any part of the vast territory within Kananaskis Country. You will have a sense of experiencing a hinterland on a visit here.

(Previous pages left) A December scene on the Highwood River shows the transition from autumn, which has left the deciduous trees bare of leaves, to winter, in which ice lines the banks of the river.

(Previous pages right) White camas, a member of the lily family, has petals with green, heart-shaped glands near the base. This species is common in dry, open situations at all elevations.

(Above) Boisterous waters run down the Highwood River in early spring.

(Right top) Trembling aspens beside the Highwood River display their September raiment of gold. On the centre skyline are snow-dusted Mt. Bishop and The Hill of the Flowers to its right. The latter feature owes its name to author R.M. Patterson.

(Right bottom) Autumn's yellows tint the deciduous trees on a symmetrical bend of the Highwood River near Fitzsimmons Creek. The river flows low and clear in fall.

99 Kananaskis Country Colours

(Above) Sunset colours create glowing clouds above the Highwood River Valley. The peaks in silhouette at the bottom of the image are {left to right from just left of centre} Mt. Muir, Mt. McPhail, an unnamed double peak north of Lake of the Horns, and Mt. Bishop.

(Right) Snow blankets the Highwood River Valley, lending a distinct seasonal aura to the landscape. Mt. Bishop {centre} and The Hill of the Flowers to its right are the predominant landmarks on the skyline.

(Above) The spruce grouse is the third species of grouse in Kananaskis Country (see pages 72--73 for the other two). This is a bird of coniferous forest, feeding mostly on spruce needles (one of the few creatures to do so). Such a spartan diet is supplemented with seeds, berries, mushrooms, and occasional insects.

(Left top) A juvenile downy woodpecker shows a red cap. This species can be distinguished from the similar hairy woodpecker by its smaller size, shorter bill, and the black marks on the white outer tail feathers. Downy woodpeckers are the smallest woodpeckers in the Canadian Rockies, but are year-round residents nonetheless, drilling out a roosting hole in which to shelter from the cold.

(Left bottom) Black-capped chickadees are among the most widespread and well-known birds in Kananaskis Country. This species has two relatives, the mountain chickadee with white eyebrows on a black cap, and the boreal chickadee with a brown cap. Chickadee calls are easily recognized, matching as they often do the sound of their name (a phenomenon known as onomatopoeia). Black-capped chickadees are hardy year-round residents, usually found in evergreens and mixed forest. They survive very cold winter nights by reducing their body temperature and shivering during sleep to generate heat, using fat reserves to fuel this high energy expenditure.

(Above) This view north from the Strawberry Hills takes in The Hill of the Flowers on the left and Mist Mountain above Odlum Ridge on the right. Open ridges such as these allow for enjoyable hiking throughout Kananaskis Country.

(Right) A typically windswept limber pine results in a dramatic silhouette on an overcast day in the Strawberry Hills. Mt. Bishop (named after Canadian First World War flying ace Billy Bishop, who won a Victoria Cross) stands grey in shadow, while sunshine highlights green meadows on The Hill of the Flowers.

(Above) Carnarvon Lake shows tropical colours in its austere basin. The name of the lake links with the 4th Earl of Carnarvon, author of the British North America Act that led to Canada's establishment as a nation in 1867. The earl also mediated disputes between British Columbia and the federal government that arose shortly after that province's entry into Confederation in 1871, so it is fitting that the lake sits almost right on the Alberta/B.C. border.

(Right top) Fall colours glow in shrubs beneath conifers. The yellows and oranges that have been hidden by the greens of active chlorophyll over summer are now revealed. The autumn reds and purples of other deciduous plants result from sugars left in the leaves.

(Right bottom) A stand of subalpine larch sweeps down from a saddle below swirling strata on Odlum Ridge. Subalpine larch, which grows only at the upper limit of trees, is a conifer but is not evergreen. Its soft, short needles turn golden in fall, then drop off, highlighting the long gnarled branches. Fresh, light green growth appears from nodes on the branches in spring.

(Above) Early morning autumn light illuminates this view from Odlum Ridge taking in Mist Mountain and its gullied eastern outlier. Victor W. Odlum was a Canadian military leader in the First World War who later served in the diplomatic corps in Australia and China.

(Right top) A multicoloured landscape between Mist Mountain and Storm Mountain is visible from Highway 40. Vegetation colonizes the gentler slopes below bare rocky ridges. At the upper limits of their range in the subalpine zone, the coniferous trees (fir and spruce) group together in island-like stands.

(Right bottom) Alpine forget-me-not.

109 Kananaskis Country Colours

(Above) A mule deer buck with its antlers budding out anew in spring. Like all male members of the deer family, antlers are cast off every year. This species is named for its large ears. Mule deer have a white rump with a cylindrical-shaped tail, white with a black tip. When fleeing quickly, mule deer use a four-legged bounding motion referred to as stotting, different from the long strides of white-tailed deer.

(Left) A white-tailed deer reaches up to feed. The white underside of the tail, part of which is visible in this image, acts as a warning signal when raised in alarm. This species is expanding its range on the eastern slopes of the Canadian Rockies, including Kananaskis Country, as human activities increase the amount of woodland edge: the habitat that white-tailed deer prefer.

(Top) Red hues in a meadow along Cataract Creek stand out in winter, a season characterized by subtlety. The view is west to the High Rock Range on the continental divide.

(Bottom) White berries contrast with fall colours in the leaves of red osier dogwood. Some of the berries still exhibit a green hue even this late in the year. The symmetrical veining of the leaves is typical of members of the dogwood family, which also includes bunchberry (dwarf dogwood) {see p. 67}. Red osier dogwood is a favourite winter browse species of moose.

Mt. Burke

Mt. Burke is the site of Cameron Lookout, which dates from 1929, making it one of the oldest fire lookouts in Alberta. Although no longer staffed, when in service it was the highest active fire lookout in Canada at 2540 metres (8330 ft) in elevation. Ironically, the height of this lookout was such that it was often in the clouds; it was eventually replaced in the 1950s by a lookout on Raspberry Ridge (the long grassy ridge visible in the mid-distance in the photograph above). The cutblocks to the left of Raspberry Ridge attest to the success of the lookouts in preventing forest fires. Both Cameron Lookout and Mt. Burke are named after pioneering ranching families.

The hike to the top of Mt. Burke begins at the Cataract Creek campground on the Forestry Trunk Road. The outing makes for a full day as the round trip distance is 16 km (10 mi) and the elevation gain tallies almost 900 metres (about 2900 ft).

One hilarious episode in the history of the lookout dates from the 1930s, when observer Murray Meister jokingly reported that he saw a battleship coming up Salter Creek. Fearing that he was going round the bend, officials ordered the rangers to take him down from his high perch. Meister's career with Forestry survived the incident, for he went on to become a ranger himself and served with the department until his retirement.

(Above) The southeast ridge of Mt. Burke gives an excellent perspective upon Plateau Mountain, whose top is indeed level but which has a number of buttresses on its periphery. The summit of this mountain was a refugia: an area that stayed ice-free during periods of glaciation. Although there are wellsites and access roads on Plateau Mountain, an ecological reserve protects features such as unusual vegetation and patterned ground (natural arrangements of rocks caused by soil churning).

(Left) The weathered shell of the Cameron fire lookout survives on the summit of Mt. Burke.

(Above) A clump of shrubby cinquefoil has put down roots in a crevice on smooth rocks beside Cataract Creek. Cultivars of this hardy and ubiquitous native member of the *Potentilla* genus are popular as ornamentals, with the benefit in addition to their beauty that wildlife are not fond of them. The name cinquefoil derives from the French *'cinque feuilles,'* referring to the usually five-parted leaves.

(Left) A crab-spider with its prey. Species of this family blend in with their host plant, and lie in wait until an unsuspecting insect such as this field crescent butterfly ventures within range. Arachnids, being eight-legged, are in a class of their own separate from the insects.

(Far left top) Stonecrop's name is appropriate as it does grow in stony ground. Like all species in its genus, this wildflower (*Sedum lanceolatum*) has fleshy leaves {unseen in this image} that store water to aid survival in its dry habitat. This adaptation is similar to that of cacti to their arid environment.

(Far left bottom) Golden bean lends its bright colour to open, dry locations in montane (low elevation) meadows in Kananaskis Country. This member of the pea family, also called buffalo bean, blooms in early spring.

(Above) A hiker pauses on the south ridge of Sentinel Peak, looking south to Hailstone Butte, which has a fire lookout on its high point.

(Left) Water plunges over a drop on Cataract Creek, an apt if generic handle. Such cascades occur where erosion has worked more slowly on resistant rock. In the Canadian Rockies, this is often dolomite, which is similar to limestone (also called calcite). In dolomite, the calcium of limestone, whose composition is calcium carbonate, has been replaced by tougher magnesium.

A dusting of snow embroiders the shady sides of these small conifers growing among shrubs in their fall palette. These meadows are in the valley of Smuts Creek: a place much frequented by moose, especially drawn to a mineral lick near Mount Engadine Lodge.

For presentation in this book, Peter Lougheed Provincial Park constitutes the fourth region of Kananaskis Country. This park, whose name honours the person instrumental in the establishment of Kananaskis Country, has a lot of infrastructure yet also holds the most rugged terrain.

Heading south on Highway 40 off the Trans-Canada Highway, you enter the park not far past Fortress Junction. The serrated Opal Range soars up to the east; although it appears forbidding, you can experience it firsthand on excursions such as the off-trail scramble of Grizzly Peak, the rockhopping-and-wading ascent of King Creek, and the bushwhack to see Opal Falls up close. Other choices include the very short Rock Glacier interpretive trail, an excellent place to observe pikas, and the well-known Ptarmigan Cirque trail near Highwood Pass, particularly spectacular in autumn when the subalpine larches turn golden.

A turn off Highway 40 leads into the facilities zone of the park, and also gives access to outings that take you away from most amenities. These include trails to a high viewpoint on Mt. Indefatigable and to Rawson Lake. In winter, cross-country skiing to Elk Pass and Blueberry Hill is a cherished tradition for many. More challenging are backpacking trips, for example to North Kananaskis Pass or on the Northover Ridge route. Higher still up the "experience required" scale are alpine climbs, such as of Mt. Joffre, highest point in Kananaskis Country.

A less-visited part of the park is that along the corridor of the gravel Smith-Dorrien/Spray Trail (Highway 742). Here are trailheads for such popular dayhikes as Chester Lake and Burstall Pass. There is also scope for off-trail scrambling, such as on The Fist, and for wildlife watching such as of moose.

This park is the jewel of Kananaskis Country and a fitting tribute to the man whose initiative led to its creation.

(Above) An off-trail scrambler strides along on the crest of Grizzly Peak, with other peaks of the Opal Range ahead to the north. The powerful geological forces of uplift and folding can be read in the steep strata, as well as the more gradual processes in which the layers of rock were first laid down as marine organisms settled at the bottom of an inland sea. Vegetation now cloaks the more gradual slopes.

(Left) Seldom-visited Opal Falls drop through a narrow notch in the Opal Range. These cascades lie east of Highway 40 near the northern junction with Valleyview Trail (an alternate gravel road that was the original highway alignment). The way to the falls is a bit of a bushwhack.

(Right) Avalanche gullies run down from the Opal Range, as seen from King Creek Ridge.

(Above) An evening vista from Gap Mountain takes in sawtooth silhouettes including {left to right} Mt. Assiniboine in the distance, Mt. Murray, and Mt. Birdwood (centre skyline). The steep off-trail scramble to the top of Gap Mountain might also reward with the sighting of a mountain goat, infrequently observed in Kananaskis Country.

(Right top) A grizzly bear feeds on fall buffaloberries just off Highway 40 near the Elbow Pass trailhead. So as not to unduly disturb the bear, this image was taken from inside my vehicle, with a window mount holding my camera and telephoto lens. The bear was busy stripping fruit and leaves from the shrubs, using its teeth and curved claws with remarkable dexterity and spending hours to ingest great quantities of berries.

(Right bottom) The shrubby plant buffaloberry (*Shepherdia canadensis*) has red or yellow fruit. The bounty of this widespread species is an important food source for many species, including bears. The berries are tart to human taste, however (thus another common name, soapberry), although Native people had various methods of preparation that mitigated the sharp flavour. Male and female buffaloberry flowers occur on separate plants.

(Above) A least chipmunk manipulates a seed with tiny forepaws. This species eats only seeds, even leaving behind the fleshy parts of fruits and berries (which other animals enjoy). Chipmunks often look comical when their cheek pouches are stuffed with food that they finish later or take back to the grassy nest. Chipmunks tap into their reserves over the winter, since they enter a state of torpor during the long interval from October to April but do wake periodically. This species is referred to as 'least' since it is the smallest of the three species of chipmunk in the Canadian Rockies. I often refer to chipmunks as having "racing stripes" since these small mammals are highly active in warm weather, often darting and scurrying to and fro. The stripes occur on both the body and the head, unlike golden-mantled ground squirrels that only have stripes on the body.

(Above) A pika shelters under an overhang. This image was taken near the Rock Glacier interpretive trail, which delves into the geological phenomenon of a slow-moving lobe-shaped mass of boulders. (Some rock glaciers had an ice core.)

Pikas

The Rock Glacier interpretive trail is an excellent spot to observe pikas (usually pronounced 'pee-ka'). You might hear one first, giving a high-pitched call that I think of as the "squeak-a of a pika." The calls can be ventriloquistic, but you'll probably soon locate the originator. It could be frozen in a pose that helps it blend in with the rocky habitat pikas prefer, although pikas have natural camouflage in that they are unobtrusive mammals, small and grey.

However, pikas, which are related to rabbits and hares (and are sometimes called 'rock rabbits'), are anything but mundane. Particularly if it's late summer, you'll likely see them scurrying about gathering vegetation. They have the intriguing behaviour of using the sun to dry their booty in what's known as a haypile, which they then stash for winter.

Despite their small size, pikas do not hibernate during the long, cold Rockies winter. Instead, they rely on the food they have cached. Pikas move about in tunnels in the snow that covers the rocks of their territories, and which has insulating properties (as the Inuit people take advantage of in building igloos).

Pikas frequent talus slopes and boulderfields with nearby plants. They know their territories well, and are often lost to sight as they dart in and out of crevices among the rocks. Although they are vulnerable to a range of predators including golden eagles, northern harriers, wolverines, and lynx, their main concerns are the small weasels. With their long cylindrical bodies, weasels can continue pursuit into the haunts of pikas. Often, though, the pikas know their home range so thoroughly that they are able to evade capture.

(Above) Reached by a short trail starting at Highwood Pass on Highway 40, Ptarmigan Cirque presents the easiest chance in the Canadian Rockies to visit such a glacially-carved basin. The ice is gone now, but the evidence of its landform-shaping power is all round. Among the signs: large boulders that were transported here and then left when the glacier melted, and small lateral moraines: ridges of material pushed up at the sides of glaciers. This hike is especially attractive in fall when the subalpine larches turn golden.

(Right) The mottled summer plumage of white-tailed ptarmigan allows them to blend in with their surroundings, then in winter they turn almost completely white to disappear against the snow. This image shows the three-toed feet, well-feathered to provide insulation to these extremities in winter. The movements of these birds from shrub to shrub in that season leave on the snow what I call a tracery of ptarmigan tracks (an alliterative allusion given that the 'p' is silent in the name).

(Above) On the west side of Highwood Pass opposite Ptarmigan Cirque lies Pocaterra Cirque, below Pocaterra Ridge (the vegetated ridge on the right). The high point on the steep grey rock of the Elk Range is known unofficially as Mt. Pocaterra. George Pocaterra (1882-1972) immigrated from Italy, arriving in Canada in 1903 with less than five dollars to his name but going on to establish the famous "Buffalo Head" ranch. A biography simply entitled *Pocaterra* appeared in 2006. Pocaterra Cirque has extensive stands of subalpine larch, and is well-known as a haunt of grizzly bears.

(Right) Fall's frosts have reddened the leaves of mountain sorrel. This member of the buckwheat family grows in sheltered spots in the alpine zone, producing small seeds in a flat round papery package.

(Above) From the top of Mt. Tyrwhitt, Upper Kananaskis Lake, Lower Kananaskis Lake, and surrounding peaks spread out beyond Elk Pass. The off-trail scramble to the top of this peak leads past a high rock arch.

(Right top) Between Highwood Ridge on the left and Grizzly Ridge on the right lie the verdant meadows of Paradise Valley. The view south encompasses the lower slopes of Mist Mountain on the left and the serrated Elk Range on the right, with a series of treed buttresses running east from its grey rocky summits.

(Right bottom) Nodding saxifrage is an alpine specialty. Note the reddish bulbets near the stem: these drop off to establish new plants of this species.

129 Kananaskis Country Colours

(Above) Late afternoon November sunlight emphasizes the jagged strata of Elpoca Mountain in a telephoto view from Highwood Pass.

(Right top) A gray jay visits a picnic table on the Pocaterra cross-country ski trail. These highly intelligent members of the corvid (crow) family readily investigate folks who pause for lunch or a break. This behaviour is merely opportunistic, since—with typical jay resourcefulness—these birds stash food for winter and are very successful in relocating all the items in their larder.

(Right bottom) A white-breasted nuthatch pauses in characteristic pose. These small forest birds, like their even smaller red-breasted cousins, often forage head-down. This feeding strategy enables nuthatches to locate items overlooked by species that use the same habitat but which forage head-up, such as woodpeckers. The nasal notes of nuthatches are heard year round in Kananaskis Country.

(Following pages) Looking west from Storm Mountain reveals this panorama over vegetated Highwood Ridge and Grizzly Ridge to the sheer-walled Elk Range on the continental divide and beyond. The glaciated peak on the right skyline is Mt. Joffre, highest point in Kananaskis Country.

(Above) A cow moose emerges with a garland on her substantial nose after immersing her head for aquatic vegetation. She is feeding in lush wetlands near the junction of the paved access road to the Kananaskis Lakes and the gravel Smith-Dorrien/Spray Trail (Highway 742).

(Right top) Fall colours prevail in this image taken at the Interlakes front-country campground on Lower Kananaskis Lake. The yellow tones include those of several stands of subalpine larch on the slopes of the Elk Range to the east.

(Right bottom) An autumn reflection at Lower Kananaskis Lake, with peaks of the Opal Range rising above a layer of mist.

135 Kananaskis Country Colours

A collage of images portraying the seasons at the Kananaskis Lakes {clockwise from the right}:

— a morel mushroom, a fungi that appears in spring;

— early blue violet, which blooms from late April to early July;

— balsam poplar leaves glow gold at Upper Kananaskis Lake, with subalpine larches on the shoulder of Mt. Sarrail on the left; and

— a cross-country ski racer competes in the Kananaskis Marathon.

(Above) The trail around Upper Kananaskis Lake grants this vista from the southeast shore. Mt. Putnik, on the left, has early autumn snow on its summit. On the right rise the rocky ramparts of the south peak of Mt. Indefatigable {see pages 140--141}.

(Right top) Narrow ribbons of water bedeck the grey walls of Mt. Sarrail above Rawson Lake. At the far end of the lake the arms of glacial moraines show where they once cradled ice. Illustrating the gradual yet inexorable process of succession, vegetation has established itself on the rocky slopes once devoid of life.

(Right bottom) Two Columbian ground squirrels poke their heads up at Rawson Lake. This elevated location confirms that this species thrives in a wide range of habitats, not only being found in the lower montane zone where it is most often observed. These small mammals excavate a well-designed complex of tunnels and chambers, including special rooms where they hibernate individually.

139 Kananaskis Country Colours

(Above) A clump of bladder locoweed persists high on the outlier east of the north peak of Mt. Indefatigable. As the name suggests, the purple flowers are replaced by large reddish seed-pods, which are swept by wind to new locations after they break off when ripe. This species is a member of the pea family.

(Left top) A classic view from the Indefatigable trail sweeps over Upper Kananaskis Lake to snow-capped peaks including Mt. Sarrail {right of centre}, with clouds lingering on the heights.

(Left bottom) The fallen cone gives the scale of twinflower. Although small, this species emits a strong sweet scent, as suggested by its membership in the honeysuckle family. The runners of twinflower, which have evergreen opposite leaves, trace across the coniferous forest floor.

(Top) You don't always get blue sky days in Kananaskis Country any more than anywhere else. On this outing, the author went for small but remote Mt. Nomad. The view is south over the approach ridge to Upper Kananaskis Lake and the peaks beyond.

(Bottom) A blustery day reveals stark and subtle shapes on the north side of Mt. Lyautey, as seen en route to Mt. Nomad.

(Right) Of course, some trips reward your efforts with exceptionally good weather, as here at Maude Lake and North Kananaskis Pass.

Northover Ridge

The challenging route over Northover Ridge represents the classic back-packing trip in Kananaskis Country. It's a demanding outing that rewards with superb views and an exhilarating sensation of expansiveness as you navigate the ridge. (Note that both these draws are contingent upon good weather.)

Having done the trip in both directions, I recommend going north to south. This has two advantages. One is that you don't have to worry so much about routefinding, in particular about the point at which to drop off the ridge if going the other way. The other benefit to heading this way is the great views of glaciated Mt. Joffre, highest peak in Kananaskis Country, which otherwise lies behind you.

(Top) The sinuous shapes of the Northover Glacier contrast with the abrupt angles of Mt. Northover, as seen on the Northover Ridge backpacking trip.

(Bottom) Backpackers on a high point near the south end of Northover Ridge savour a stupendous panorama, in which massive Mt. Joffre with its impressively glaciated north face is the outstanding highlight.

(Left) Looking west to Defender Mountain and the Royal Group {both in British Columbia} from above the saddle at the north end of Northover Ridge.

(Above) Aster Lake beckons on a fine autumn day. It is a tough slog to get to this remote spot, but the effort is compensated with alpine surroundings that invite further exploration. The backcountry campground here is the usual base for the climb of Mt. Joffre {see pages 148--149}, and is used by most parties doing the Northover Ridge trip.

(Left) Roseroot, a rare wildflower normally found in the alpine zone, forms red seedpods. This member of the *Sedum* genus has fleshy leaves that store moisture, a beneficial adaptation in its rocky habitat.

(Top) The view west from near the summit of Mt. Sarrail extends over Aster Lake to {left to right in the mid-distance} Warrior Mountain, Mt. Northover, and Mt. Lyautey. Beyond are the more heavily glaciated peaks of the Royal Group, with numerous other ranges off to the horizon.

(Bottom) Alpine cinquefoil, which belongs to the rose family, lends a splash of colour to rocky terrain.

Mt. Joffre

At 3450 metres (11,319 ft) in elevation, glaciated Mt. Joffre stands as the highest point in Kananaskis Country. It ranks in the top 30 peaks by height in the Canadian Rockies, and is the highest mountain between Mt. Assiniboine and the United States border.

The name of Mt. Joffre is not particularly linked with its location, for it was given in honour of a French general of the First World War. (Many of the peak names in the area have a similar derivation, or are after warships.) The first ascent of Mt. Joffre was made in 1919 by Joseph Hickson and Edward Feuz, Jr., his Swiss-born guide. Hickson, a McGill University professor, was one of the few Canadians who played a major role in early Rockies mountaineering. Among his other first ascents was that of nearby Mt. Sir Douglas, at 3406 metres (11,174 ft) the second-highest point in Kananaskis Country.

Our party of four almost didn't even get started on our attempt, since heavy rain was pouring down as we drove to the trailhead at Upper Kananaskis Lake. However, the deluge let up in mid-afternoon, so we dashed up the steep route to Aster Lake. Snow lingered at the campsite but the white stuff made for ideal conditions the next day once on the mountain proper.

A suitably alpine start at 4 a.m., requiring headlamps, got us off and away. Roping up on the Mangin Glacier (named after another First World War military figure), our ascent of Mt. Joffre took the North Face. We put in perfect switchbacks up the snowy ramp, set at an angle of about 40 degrees.

Our stay at the top of Mt. Joffre was brief due to a cool wind, but after savouring some bumslide glissades on the descent we stripped down to short sleeves once off the glacier. We indulged in some hijinks on the way back to camp, and hung around a while soaking up the ambiance in the glow of our successful ascent. Then we blitzed down from Aster Lake, arriving back at the car not much more than 24 hours after setting out.

It had been an intense and rewarding jaunt. At the end I launched into my rendition of a variation of a Rolling Stones song: "I know it's only rock and snow, but I like it, I like it, yes I do!"

(Above) My three ropemates on the climb {left to right} Justin Steele, Chris Shannon, and Brendan Ross, celebrate on the summit of Mt. Joffre on an ideal July day in 2003.

(Left) Chris Shannon pauses on the Mangin Glacier during the ascent. On the left skyline, beyond castellated Mt. Mangin, are summits of the Royal Group in British Columbia's Height of the Rockies Provincial Park. Mt. Sir Douglas, the high peak near the centre skyline, reaches the second-highest elevation in Kananaskis Country after Mt. Joffre.

(Above) A vista over Chester Lake and beyond to Mt. Birdwood {centre} and Mt. Smuts {right} is the reward of venturing above the southeast shore. The shallows of the lake reveal a turquoise shade, looking tropical, which feels almost right on a sunny summer day such as this, but the impression is belied by the fact that the lake freezes over in winter and you can cross-country ski on it.

(Left top) The route to the austere Black Prince Lakes passes through this luxuriant meadow below the north face of Mt. Warspite.

(Left bottom) Warspite Cascades tumble down near the rough trail on the way to the meadow below Mt. Warspite.

(Above) A late September hike on the Burstall Pass trail finds the subalpine larches still glowing gold. From not far below the pass, this sweeping vista takes in {left to right} Mt. Birdwood and its eastern subpeak (referred to as Sharks Tooth), Commonwealth Peak, and snowy Mt. Galatea on the other side of the valley from the trailhead.

(Right top) Off-trail scramblers negotiate a ridge near South Burstall Pass, with Mt. Sir Douglas soaring above.

(Right bottom) An eye-catching fossilized snail {gastropod}.

153 Kananaskis Country Colours

(Above) A single subalpine larch stands sentinel in September on the crest of Burstall Pass. Whistling Rock Ridge, the end of the long north ridge of Mt. Sir Douglas, stands in dark contrast to swirling white clouds.

(Left top) Cirrus clouds sweep across the sky above the valley in the vicinity of the Burstall Pass trailhead, with Commonwealth Peak in the upper right.

(Left bottom) A hoary marmot, which gives shrill piercing alarm calls. These gregarious mammals graze frequently when active, but hibernate for two-thirds of each year.

(Above) Off-trail scramblers approach the steep, narrow gully, to the left of the fin of rock, which is the key to the non-technical ascent of the peak known as The Fist. The name comes from its shape as seen from the east.

(Right top) On the descent of The Fist, shortly below the summit, some members of the party get a belay on an exposed section. Tryst Lake lies far below.

(Right bottom) Shadows fill the valley of Commonwealth Creek as members of an off-trail scrambling party prepare to end a long day by returning into that valley and hiking back out. Mt. Birdwood rises dramatically on the right, with Commonwealth Peak (another scrambling objective) on the left skyline.

157 Kananaskis Country Colours

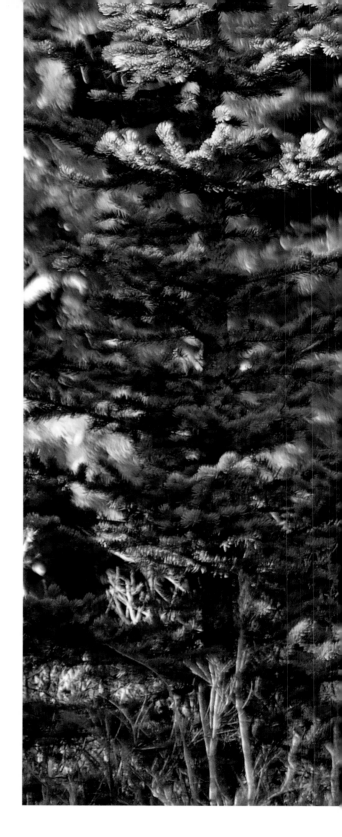

(Above) A massive bull moose makes its way through forest, little impeded by its huge antlers. This animal is headed for a mineral lick near the junction of the Smith-Dorrien/Spray Trail (Highway 742) and the road to the Mt. Shark helipad and trailhead. Several moose at once can often be observed at this lick, which is within easy viewing distance for guests staying at Mount Engadine Lodge.

(Left) A beautifully-coloured Steller's jay perches attentively on a lodgepole pine branch. This species, named after an early naturalist, is a year-round but uncommon resident in Kananaskis Country.

Further Reading

Acorn, John, *Bugs of Alberta* (Lone Pine Publishing, Edmonton, 2000).

Acorn, John, *Butterflies of Alberta* (Lone Pine Publishing, Edmonton, 1993).

Acorn, John, *Damselflies of Alberta: Flying Neon Toothpicks in the Grass* (University of Alberta Press, Edmonton, 2004).

Corbett, Bill, *The 11,000ers of the Canadian Rockies* (Rocky Mountain Books, Calgary, 2004).

Daffern, Gillean, *Canmore and Kananaskis Country: Short Walks for Enquiring Minds Volume 1, second edition* (Rocky Mountain Books, Calgary, 2003).

Daffern, Gillean, *Kananaskis Country Trail Guide Volume 1, third edition* (Rocky Mountain Books, Calgary, 1996).

Daffern, Gillean, *Kananaskis Country Trail Guide Volume 2, third edition* (Rocky Mountain Books, Calgary, 1997).

Finch, David, *R.M. Patterson: A Life of Great Adventure* (Rocky Mountain Books, Calgary, 2000).

Gadd, Ben, *Handbook of the Canadian Rockies, second edition* (Corax Press, Jasper, 1995).

Hallworth, Beryl & C.C. Chinnappa, *Plants of Kananaskis Country in the Rocky Mountains of Alberta* (The University of Calgary Press, Calgary, 1997).

Hamblin, Jennifer and David Finch, *Pocaterra* (Rocky Mountain Books, Calgary, 2006).

Heinrich, Bernd, *Winter World: The Ingenuity of Animal Survival* (HarperCollins Publishers, New York, 2003).

Kane, Alan, *Scrambles in the Canadian Rockies, third edition* (Rocky Mountain Books, Calgary, 1999).

Marriott, John, *Central Rockies Mammals, second edition* (Luminous Compositions, Calgary, 2005).

Patterson, R.M., *The Buffalo Head* (TouchWood Editions {formerly Horsdal & Schubart Publishers}, Victoria, 2001 [first published by William Sloane Associates, New York, 1961]).

Potter, Mike, *Central Rockies Placenames* (Luminous Compositions, Calgary, 1997).

Potter, Mike, *Central Rockies Wildflowers, second edition* (Luminous Compositions, Calgary, 2005).

Potter, Mike, *Fire Lookout Hikes in the Canadian Rockies* (Luminous Compositions, Calgary, 1998).

Potter, Mike, *Ridgewalks in the Canadian Rockies, second printing* (Luminous Compositions, Calgary, 2003).

Potter, Mike, *White Wilderness: The Canadian Rockies in Winter* (Luminous Compositions, Calgary, 2001).

Sibley, David Allen, *The Sibley Guide to Birds* (Alfred A. Knopf, New York, 2000).